I0868371

CHINESE FESTIVALS

The Mid-Autumn Festival

Edited by Li Chaodong

Translated by Daniel Jingyuan Ni

RC

Books Beyond Boundaries

ROYAL COLLINS

"People have happiness and sorrows, and the moon waxes and wanes." The bright moon high in the sky has a rich cultural connotation. The one most closely related to the moon is the traditional Chinese festival: the Mid-Autumn Festival.

The fifteenth day of the eighth lunar month is the Mid-Autumn Festival. According to the ancient Chinese calendar, there are four seasons in a year, three months per season, which is called "Mengyue, Zhongyue, Jiyue," meaning the first, the second, and the third month, respectively. So the second month of autumn is called "Zhongqiu." And the 15th day of the eighth lunar month falls in the middle of that month, so it is called the "Mid-Autumn Festival."

The origin of the Mid-Autumn Festival is related to the natural worship of the Chinese ancestors. The ancients formulated the calendar according to the law of the moon's waxing and waning, the temperature change of the four seasons, as well as the solar terms to guide farming life. Autumn is the season for harvest. By then, people hold activities to worship the moon, celebrate the harvest, and thank nature for its gifts.

Chinese emperor offering sacrifices to the moon

As early as the Zhou Dynasty (1046–256 BC), emperors had the custom of offering sacrifices to the moon on Autumn Equinox. In the Ming Dynasty (AD 1368–1644), the royal family even built a place exclusively for offering sacrifices to the moon, now known as "Yue Tan" (Moon Altar) in Beijing.

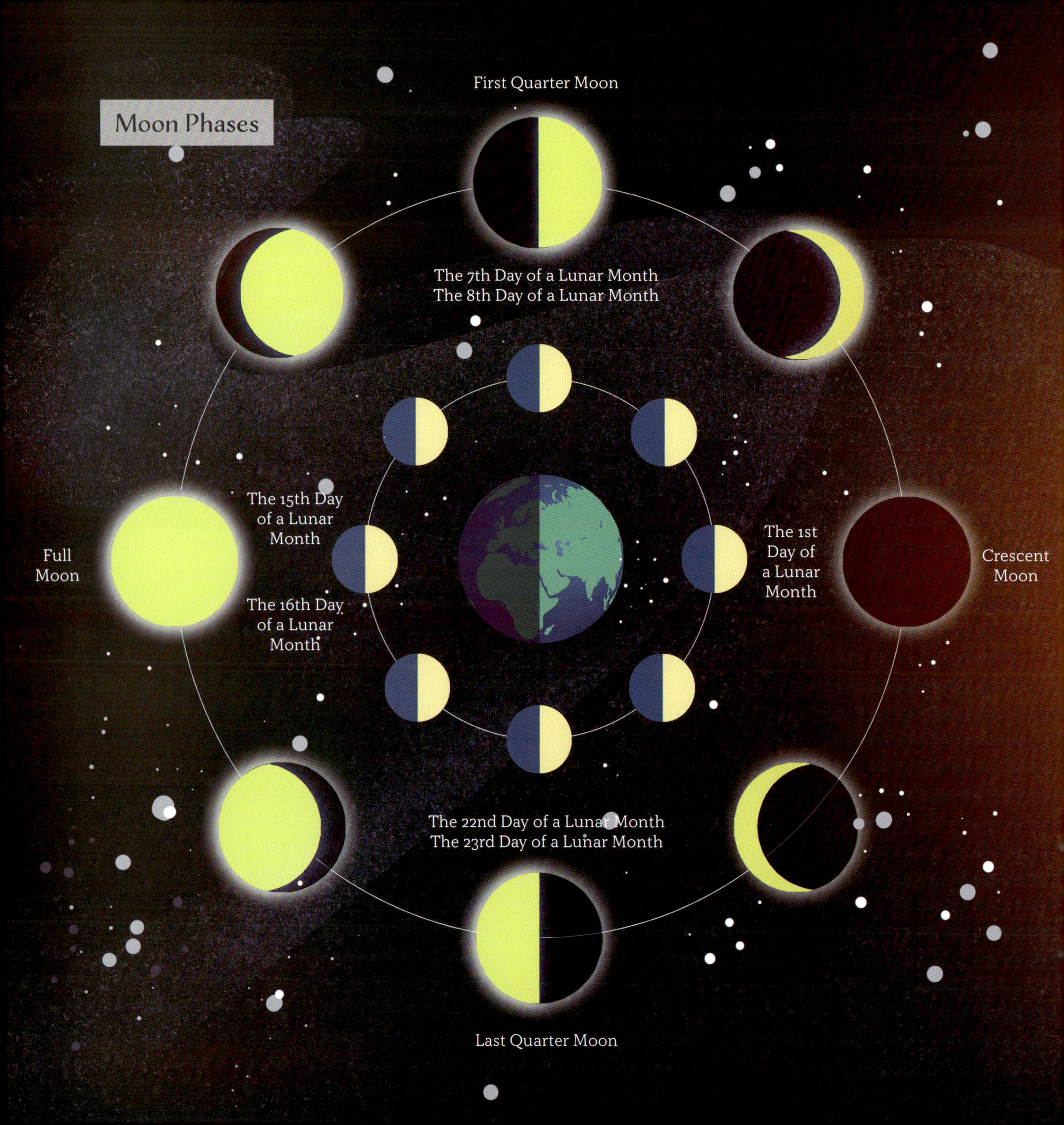
Moon Phases
First Quarter Moon
The 7th Day of a Lunar Month
The 8th Day of a Lunar Month
The 15th Day of a Lunar Month
The 16th Day of a Lunar Month
Full Moon
The 1st Day of a Lunar Month
Crescent Moon
The 22nd Day of a Lunar Month
The 23rd Day of a Lunar Month
Last Quarter Moon

The moon itself does not shine but only reflects sunlight. Generally speaking, the earth is between the sun and the moon on the fifteenth or sixteenth day of a lunar month. The side of the moon facing the earth is full of sunlight. From the perspective of the earth, the moon is shiny and round.
In August, the temperature drops, the water vapor in the atmosphere decreases, the transparency increases, and the moonlight is extremely bright. That's why the moon at the Mid-Autumn Festival is big, round, and bright.
Dad, why does the moon at the Mid-Autumn Festival look so big, round, and bright?

The ancients also produced many myths related to the moon, the most famous of which was "Chang'e (a Chinese mythological figure) Rushes to the Moon."

According to Chinese legend, one year in ancient times, ten suns appeared in the sky and burned the ground to smoke, making it hard for people to live.

There was an extremely powerful hero named Hou Yi, who was determined to relieve the people of this suffering. He climbed to the top of Kunlun Mountain. Drawing his divine bow to the full, Hou Yi shot nine suns in one breath. Many people respected him and came to learn from him.

In order to thank Hou Yi, Xi Wangmu* gave Hou Yi a pill of immortal medicine. He gave the medicine to his wife, Chang'e, for safekeeping. Everyone liked Chang'e very much because she was a beautiful and kind woman who often helped the villagers.

* A goddess of Chinese mythology and folk belief.

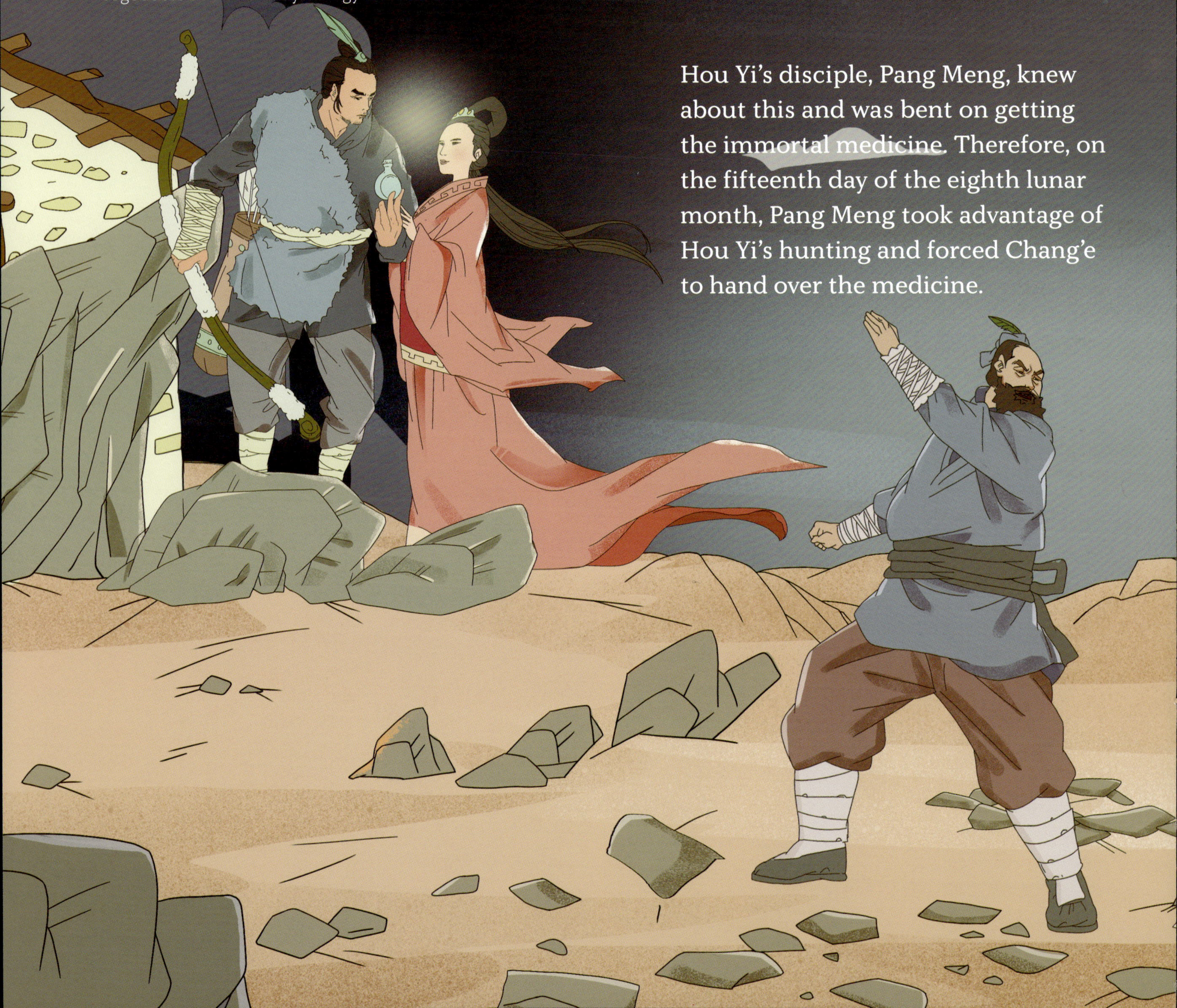

Hou Yi's disciple, Pang Meng, knew about this and was bent on getting the immortal medicine. Therefore, on the fifteenth day of the eighth lunar month, Pang Meng took advantage of Hou Yi's hunting and forced Chang'e to hand over the medicine.

To fail Pang Meng's attempt, Chang'e swallowed the immortal medicine in one bite. Suddenly she floated off the ground, flew to the sky, and finally fell onto the moon.

Back from his outing and getting to know what happened, Hou Yi was heartbroken. Missing his wife, he went to the back garden Chang'e loved to stay and set up an incense table. He put the desserts and fresh fruit she loved on the incense table and made round mooncakes (a Chinese-style pastry), showing his wish for a reunion and looking forward to Chang'e's return.

The villagers missed the kind Chang'e and set up incense tables under the moon to pray for the kind Chang'e, wishing her peace and good luck.

Although the "Moon Worship" of the ancestors appeared very early in history, it took a long for the Mid-Autumn Festival in the modern sense to come into being.

During the Tang Dynasty (AD 618–907), it became quite popular among scholars to admire and appreciate the moon's beauty. They chanted poems to the moon while enjoying the full moon. In the writings of the literati, the moon became people's emotional sustenance, colored with a romantic sense.

In the Song Dynasty (AD 960–1279), worshipping the moon and expressing affection for the moon became a dominant way for people to express their desire for reunion, recreation, and happiness.

Cup aloft, beckoning
moon's embrace,
My shadow and I, her
third in grace.

The Tang and Song dynasties were an era of ethnic migration and integration. People connected the moon with their hometowns, relatives, and friends, and the meaning of reunion began to appear during the Mid-Autumn Festival. In the Northern Song Dynasty (AD 960–1127), the imperial court officially designated the fifteenth day of the eighth lunar month the Mid-Autumn Festival.

In the ancient philosophy of Yin-Yang, the moon belongs to Yin and is in charge of birth-giving. So women were more enthusiastic about the tradition of moon worship. According to the legend, Chang'e, the goddess on the moon, is beautiful and kind. The girls worship the moon, hoping to be as beautiful as Chang'e on the moon!

There is also a small taboo for moon worshipping during the Mid-Autumn Festival. Children can't point to the moon with their fingers. Otherwise, their ears will be cut by the Moon God (not Chang'e). In fact, the original intention is to let children learn to respect the gods of heaven and earth.

"The moon on the fifteenth day of the eighth lunar month is full, and the Mid-Autumn Festival mooncakes are fragrant and sweet." Mooncakes symbolize reunion and reflect people's good wishes for family reunions. Today, there are various mooncakes in different forms and flavors.

Beijing-Style Mooncake

Moderately sweet, crispy, flaky, and oily.

Teochow*-Style Mooncake

The skin is crispy, and the filling is fine, oily but not fatty, and sweet but not greasy.

* A city in eastern Guangdong Province.

Quzhou*-Style Mooncake

Sesame is the main raw material, so Quzhou-style mooncakes are also known as Quzhou Sesame Cakes.

* A city located in the lower reaches of the Yangtze River.

Cantonese-Style Mooncake

With a thin crust and large filling, the color is golden, the pattern is exquisite, and the taste is soft and smooth.

Suzhou-Style Mooncake

The skin is crispy and loose. The mooncakes can be sweet or salty, roasted or baked. Shanghai fresh meat mooncakes are well received.

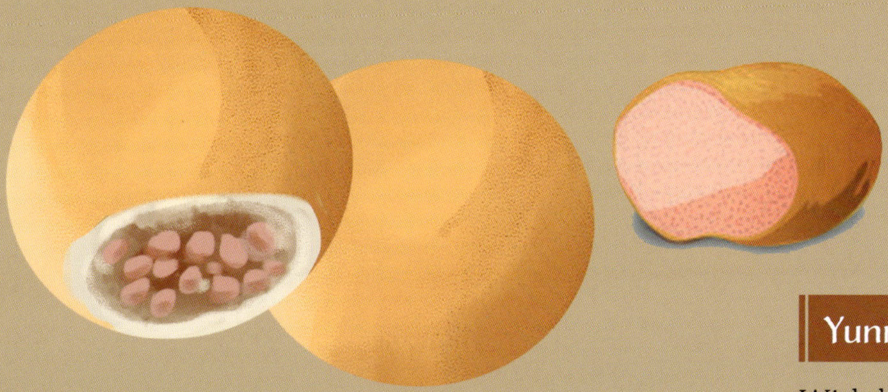

Yunnan-Style Mooncake

With ham and flowers as fillings, the crust is loose, the filling is salty and sweet, and rose flower cakes are widely favored.

In addition to mooncakes, seasonal fruits, and other foods are the achievements of autumn harvest in farming society and thus become indispensable festival food.

Osmanthus Cake, Osmanthus Wine

When osmanthus is blooming and fragrant, people eat osmanthus cakes and drink osmanthus wine.

Grapefruit

Grapefruits are eaten during the Mid-Autumn Festival in Guangxi. “Grapefruit” in Chinese is pronounced as “You,” which sounds like another Chinese character meaning blessing. So people eat grapefruits hoping the moon god to bless them.

Watermelon

Shaanxi people eat watermelons during the Mid-Autumn Festival because the shape of the watermelon is round, symbolizing reunion. Watermelons should also be cut into the shape of a lotus, which means festive and auspicious.

Water Chestnut

Eating water chestnuts at the Mid-Autumn Festival is said to make children smart because it is pronounced similar to another character meaning smart.

River Snail

Eating river snails around the Mid-Autumn Festival is popular in Guangdong. August is the time for snails to be nonpregnant. No small snails are in the abdomen, and the meat is particularly tasty.

Pomegranate

In a pomegranate, the red seeds are like agate, white seeds as crystals. While eating, it tastes like crystalline jade blasting juice. It also symbolizes longevity, reunion, and auspiciousness.

Pear

Eating pears means "being not separate."

Lotus-Root Sandwich

People from Jiangsu and Zhejiang eat lotus root during the Mid-Autumn Festival. The lotus roots are mostly made into round cakes, which means reunion.

Pumpkin

People in the southern area of the Yangtze River eat warm and sweet pumpkins during the Mid-Autumn Festival.

Hairy Crab

"The autumn wind rises, and the crab's feet are itchy; chrysanthemums bloom and attract the crabs." This is a Chinese proverb to the effect that during autumn, when chrysanthemums are in full bloom, hairy crabs reach their peak of fertility as the wind blows. It is the best time to taste crabs around the Mid-Autumn Festival since the crabs are full of crab roe and cream.

Taro

Chaoshan people eat taro during the Mid-Autumn Festival, hoping to have good luck.

Reunion Bun

It is a must-eat traditional food for the Mid-Autumn Festival in Xi'an, Shaanxi Province. The whole family eats one steamed bun.

Maijian (a flour-coated meat or vegetable filling and steamed food)

It is a kind of festival food eaten during the Mid-Autumn Festival in Shandong.

In addition to worshipping the moon, appreciating the moon, and eating mooncakes, different Mid-Autumn Festival customs have also been formed in various places.

In Beijing, the “Master Rabbit” is one of the symbols of the Mid-Autumn Festival. These clay toys of different shapes and sizes are very popular among children.

In Zhejiang, admiring the Qiantang River tide can be said to be another Mid-Autumn Festival event.

"The mid-autumn moon shines its light over thousands of miles; the sound of midnight tide seems like tens and thousands of soldiers' mounting a charge against the enemies."

When the moon is full, gravity is the greatest, bringing tides rolling all over, which can be described as an amazing spectacle.

Orange lanterns (by digging out the oranges and lighting candles inside) are lit in some places in Sichuan. They are hung out at the doorway to celebrate the festival.

There are also children inserting incense on grapefruit and dancing along the street, which is called "dancing with fragrant meteor ball." The fragrant grapefruit, when lit, looks like a meteor, and children play and dance with it.

Minorities also hold distinctive folk activities during the Mid-Autumn Festival.

For example, the Mongolian "chasing the moon." The persistent Mongolian riders keep chasing until the moon goes down in the west.

Another example is the "Moon Dance" by Miao, Yi, and other minorities. Enthusiastic people sing and dance to their heart's content in the moonlight.

The Mid-Autumn Festival is celebrated not only in China but also in some East and Southeast Asia countries. The Republic of Korea calls the Mid-Autumn Festival "Autumn Eve," a day to sweep tombs and offer sacrifices to the ancestors with newly harvested grains and fruits. There is a custom of dancing in circles and eating muffins.

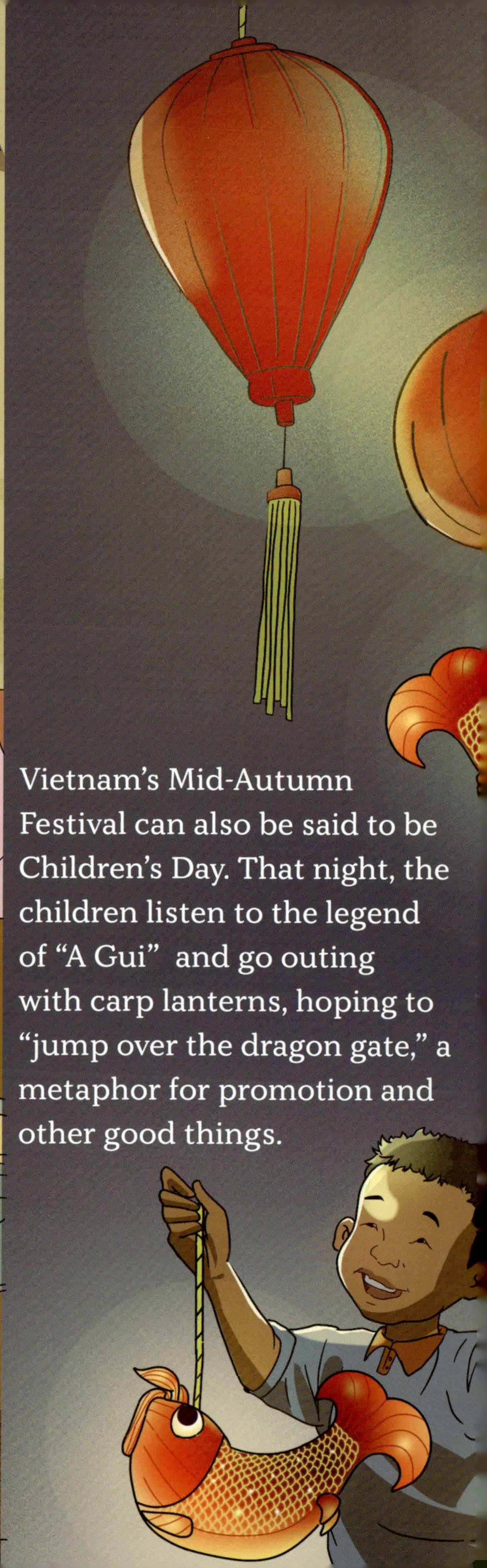

Vietnam's Mid-Autumn Festival can also be said to be Children's Day. That night, the children listen to the legend of "A Gui" and go outing with carp lanterns, hoping to "jump over the dragon gate," a metaphor for promotion and other good things.

Japan calls the Mid-Autumn Festival the "Fifteenth Night," on which people will admire the moon, eat rice balls, and hold various celebrations.

"One Mid-Autumn Festival every year, the full moon cures the homesickness."

The Mid-Autumn Festival originated from a farming society. It is a festival to celebrate a bumper harvest and express gratitude for nature. It contains the natural thought of the unity of humans and nature. After a long historical accumulation, it has become one of the most valued and popular festivals by Chinese people, second only to Chinese New Year.

From the sacrificial etiquette showing reverence for heaven and earth to the symbol of family reunion, it is not difficult for us to see the importance of the full moon hanging high in the sky for the Chinese people—in whatever era it contains people's love for present life and yearning for future life.

CHINESE FESTIVALS

The Mid-Autumn Festival

Edited by Li Chaodong
Translated by Daniel Jingyuan Ni

First published in 2023 by Royal Collins Publishing Group Inc.
Groupe Publication Royal Collins Inc.
BKM Royalcollins Publishers Private Limited

Headquarters: 550-555 boul. René-Lévesque O Montréal (Québec) H2Z1B1 Canada
India office: 805 Hemkunt House, 8th Floor, Rajendra Place, New Delhi 110 008

Original Edition © Hohai University Press

All rights reserved. Without limiting the rights under copyright reserved above, no part of this publication may be reproduced, stored in or introduced into a retrieval system, or transmitted in any form or by any means (electronic, mechanical, photocopying, recording or otherwise), without the prior written permission of both the copyright owner and the above publisher of this book.

ISBN: 978-1-4878-1154-9

To find out more about our publications, please visit www.royalcollins.com.

ABOUT THE EDITOR

Li Chaodong, born in 1963, graduated from the Department of History of East China Normal University. He is a famous education publisher in China. He has edited and published more than 50 sets of books. He has won the title of "National Leading Talent in Press and Publication" and "China's Annual Publication Figure." He is the Founding Vice President of the All-China Federation of Industry and Commerce Book Industry Chamber of Commerce, Vice President of the Fifth Council of the Books and Periodicals Distribution Association of China, Vice Chairman of Anhui Publishing Association, and Vice Chairman of Jiangsu Publishing Association.